CANADIAN CONTEMPORARY REPERTOIRE SERIES

FUN SELECTIONS OF JAZZ - POP - LATIN - FOLK

LEVEL FIVE

CONSERVATORY CANADA™

For more information about Conservatory Canada
and its programs visit our website at:
www.conservatorycanada.ca

Office of the Registrar
Conservatory Canada
45 King Street, S
London, Ontario,
N6A 1B8

T0078901

FONDATION

SOCAN
FOUNDATION

© 2011 Conservatory Canada
Published and Distributed by Novus Via Music Group Inc.
All Rights Reserved.

ISBN 978-1-49500-540-4

Novus Via Music Group Inc.
189 Douglas Street, Stratford, Ontario, Canada N5A 5P8
(519) 273-7520 www.NVmusicgroup.com

Preface

Canadian Contemporary Repertoire Series: Fun Selections of Jazz, Pop, Latin and Folk Music Level Five is an exciting series of piano works by Canadian composers. Level Five offers grade five and six students twenty-two appealing pieces at varied levels within the grade requirement. Students will develop technical and musical skills with user-friendly repertoire from an entrance level to grade six works.

Repertoire selections have been based on grade appropriate keys, time signatures, accompaniment figures, degree of difficulty and length. Jazz styles include preparatory rags like *Little Buzz Rag*, which leads comfortably to similar challenges presented by *Vaquero*, in a completley different style. *Barefoot Boogie, Bumblebee in Lavender, Clements' Lament* and *Diggin' In Blues* provide varied accompaniments and blues scale playing. Students will be delighted by the swing rhythm of works like *Ambling Along, Jazz Study No. 1* and *Paige's Turn*. The lovely jazz ballad *Sheri's Song*, jazz prelude *Into the Sunrise* and jazz waltz *Waltz of the Water Sprites* are just some of the jazz titles offered in this collection.

The ever popular work *Sun Flower Slow Drag* has also been included in this collection. Students will be rockin' to titles like *Rock Bottom* and *Reggae,* while Latin dance rhythms are included in works like *Tango for My Lovely Mom* and *Demasiado Tango.* Arrangements of folk songs *The Moody B'ys* and *Ev'ry Night When the Sun Goes Down* provide a strong sense of Canadian and spiritual musical heritage.

Conservatory Canada wants to keep music students studying longer! We understand the benefits gained through the study of music and we believe that students will remain engaged and excited about their studies if that music is current and familiar.

This is why we developed the Contemporary Idioms curriculum. Students can now be assessed and accredited through a program that involves contemporary styles of music such as Swing, Blues, Latin and Rock.

Conservatory Canada supports Canadian composers. This book contains pieces that are either original compositions or arrangements by Canadian musicians. All the selections in this book are eligible for a Conservatory Canada Contemporary Idioms examination. The pieces have been chosen with attention to proper pedagogy, skill development and student appeal. We hope you enjoy them!

TABLE OF CONTENTS

Own Choice

Clements' Lament	Brian W. Usher	10
Ev'ry Night When the Sun Goes Down	Wolfgang Bottenberg (arr)	16
Into the Sunrise	Brian W. Usher	22
Sheri's Song	Andrew Harbridge	36
The Moody B'ys	Debra Wanless (arr)	46
Waltz of the Water Sprites	Sheila Tyrrell	48

Rock/Latin

Demasiado Tango	David Story	12
Detroit is Rockin'	David Story	14
Diggin' In Blues	Tyler Seidenberg	18
Rock Bottom	Karen Rowell	19
Vaquero	Andrew Harbridge	31
Swamp Rock	Tyler Seidenberg	42
Tango For My Lovely Mom	Fishel Pustilnik	44

Swing

Ambling Along	Karen Rowell	4
Bumblebee in Lavender	Joyce Pinckney (arr)	8
Jazz Study No. 1	Nicholas Fairbank	24
Paige's Turn	Brian W. Usher	28
Stayin' Cool	Karen Rowell	38

Traditional

Barefoot Boogie	Diane Hunter	6
Little Buzz Rag	Diane Hunter	26
Reggae	Andrew Harbridge	34
Sun Flower Slow Drag	Debra Wanless (arr)	40

Ambling Along

Karen Rowell

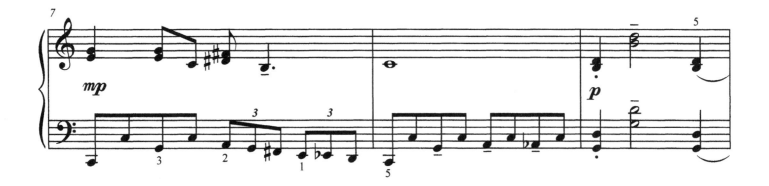

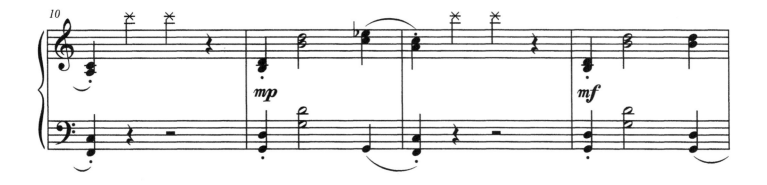

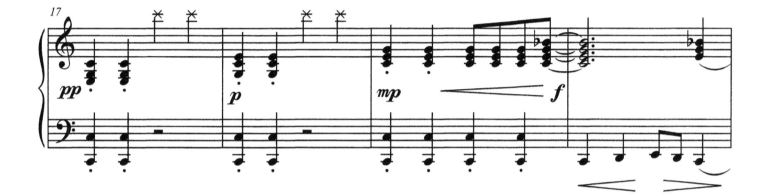

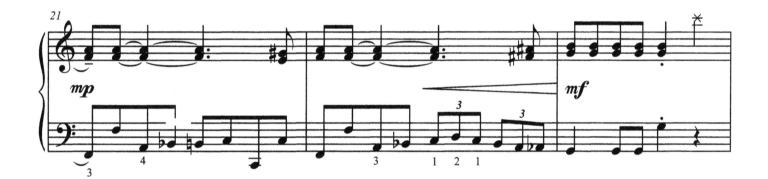

An "x" note means to knock the piano with your knuckles in that rhythm.

Barefoot Boogie

Diane Hunter

Happy Fingers

Bumblebee in Lavender

arr. Joyce Pinckney

Buzzily

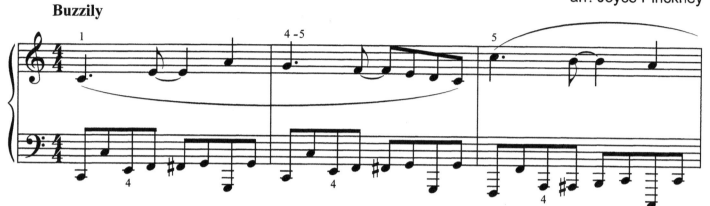

Lazily, with a swing

Clements' Lament

for Professor Peter Clements

Brian W. Usher

Improvise using
given notes on chords

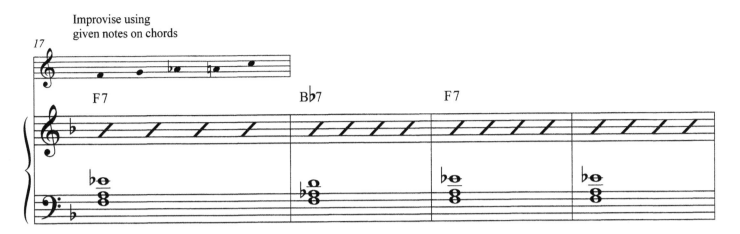

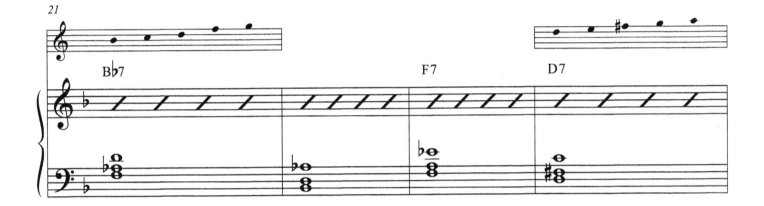

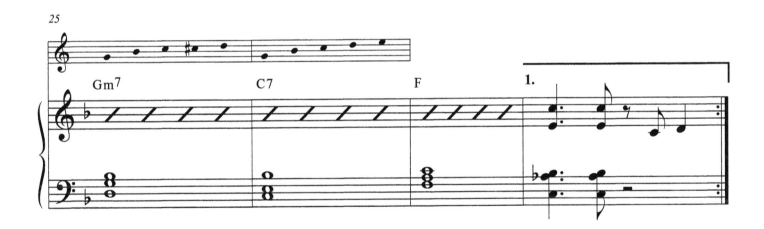

Clement's Lament 2 / 2

Demasiado Tango

David Story

To Coda ⊕

Improvise on G minor harmonic scale
mf ad lib. dynamics

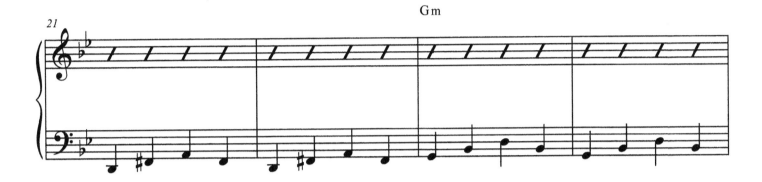

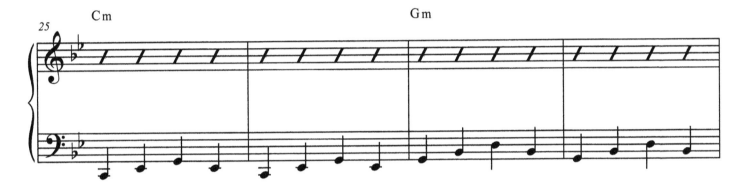

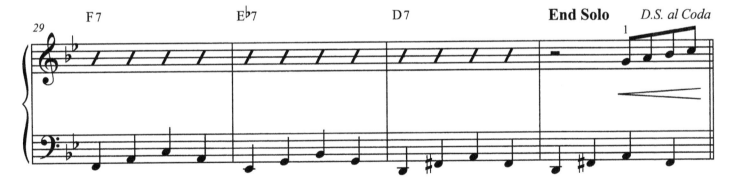

End Solo   *D.S. al Coda*

Coda ⊕

Ad lib fills

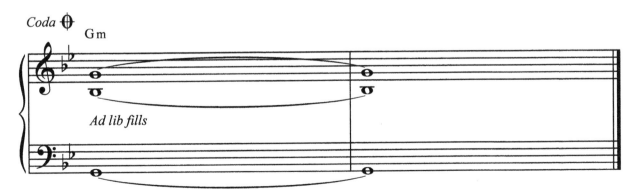

Detroit is Rockin'

David Story

Detroit is Rockin' 2 / 2

Ev'ry Night When the Sun Goes Down

arr. Wolfgang Bottenberg

Medium Blues Tempo

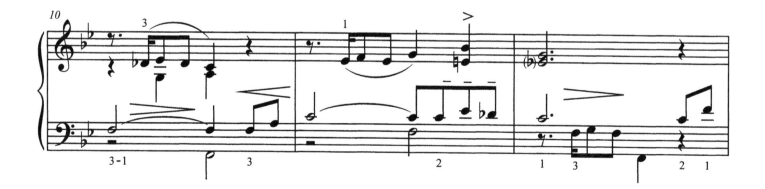

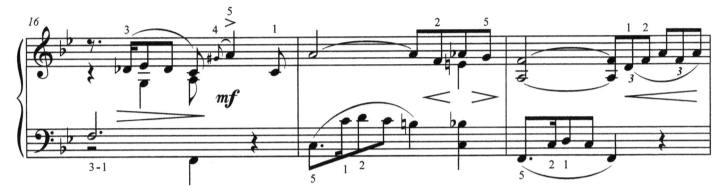

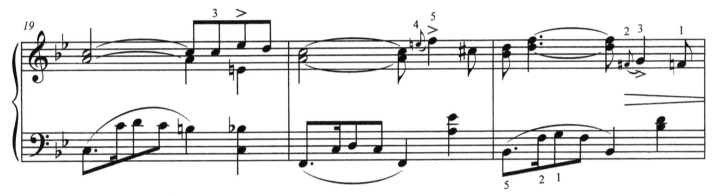

Ev'ry Night When the Sun Goes Down 2 / 2

Diggin' In Blues

Accented and groovy

Tyler Seidenberg

Rock Bottom

Karen Rowell

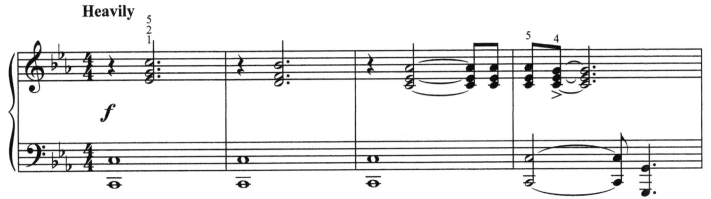

Small hands may omit the top note of the octave bass line.

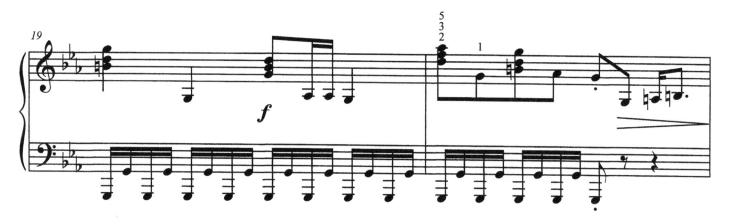

Rock Bottom 3 / 3

Into the Sunrise

Brian W. Usher

Molto espressivo

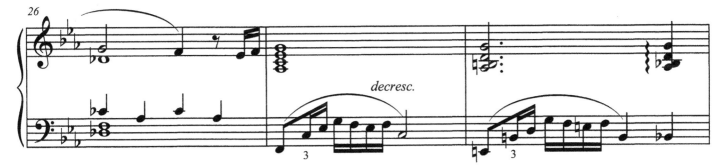

Into the Sunrise 2 / 2

Jazz Study No.1

Nicholas Fairbank

Moderate Swing

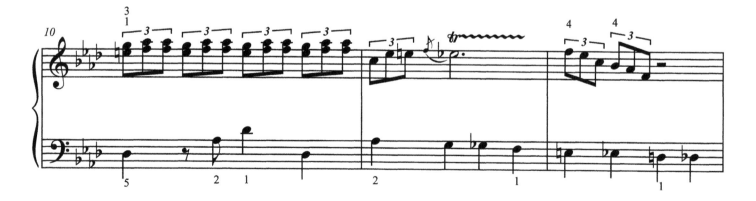

Jazz Study No.1   2 / 2

Little Buzz Rag

My Dog

Diane Hunter

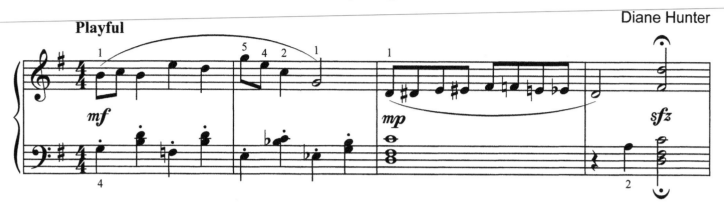

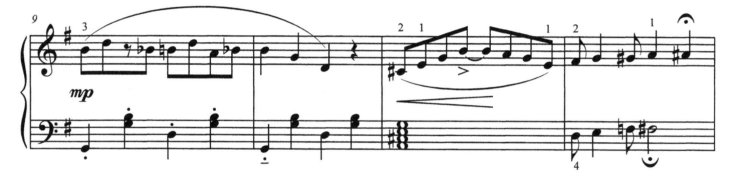

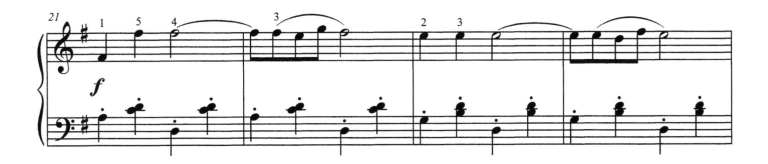

Little Buzz Rag   2 / 2

Paige's Turn

Brian W. Usher

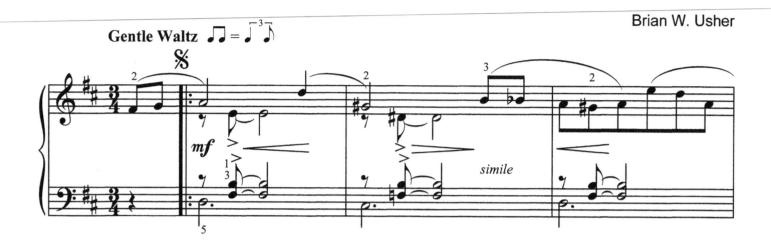

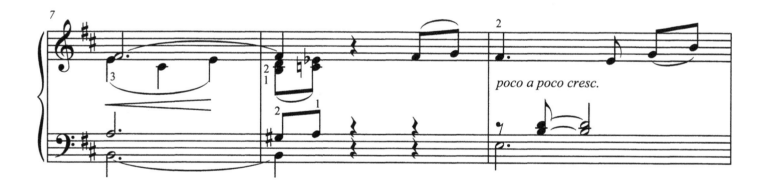

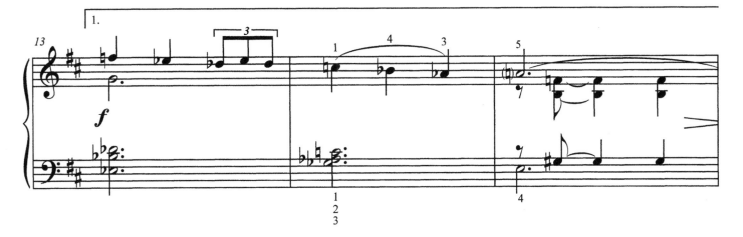

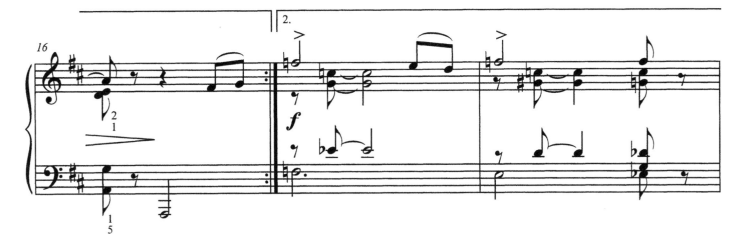

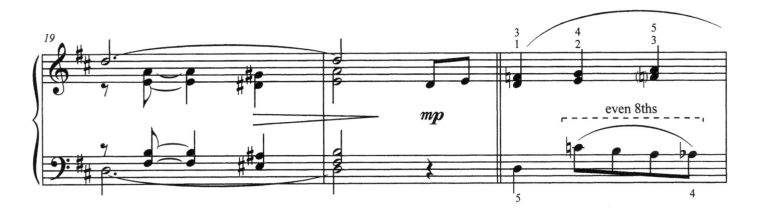

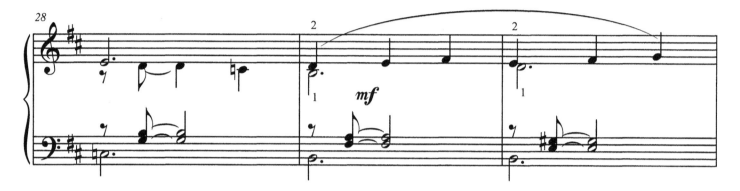

D.S. al Coda

Vaquero

Andrew Harbridge

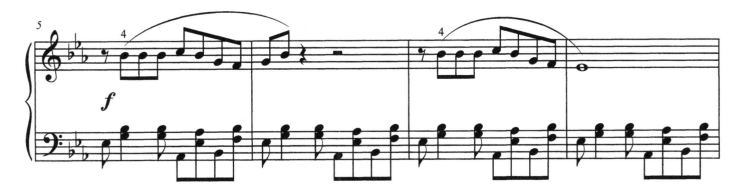

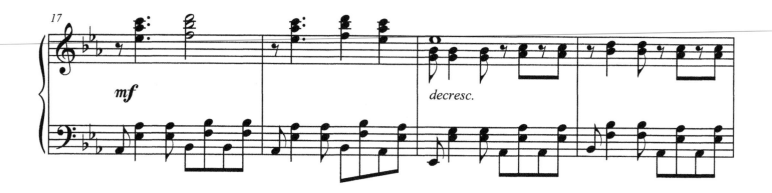

Vaquero 3 / 3

Reggae

Andrew Harbridge

With a reggae feel (swing the 8ths slightly)

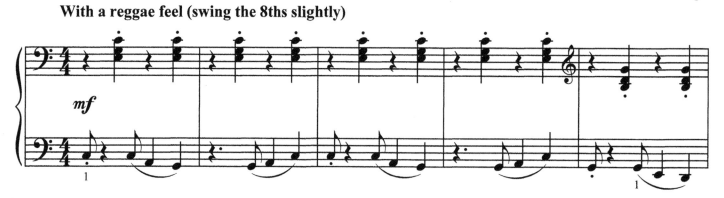

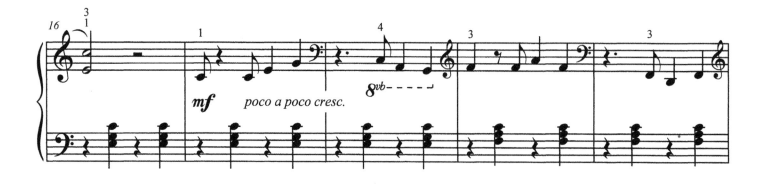

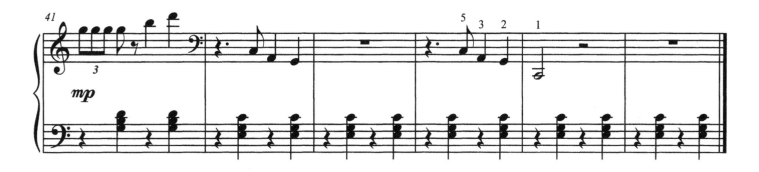

Reggae 2 / 2

Sheri's Song

Andrew Harbridge

Andante cantabile

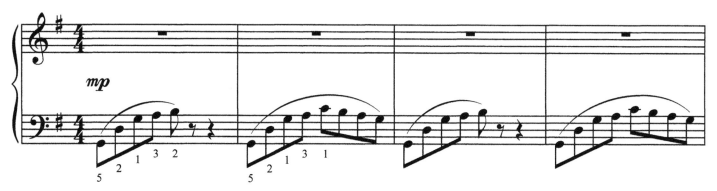

Sheri's Song 2 / 2

Stayin' Cool

Karen Rowell

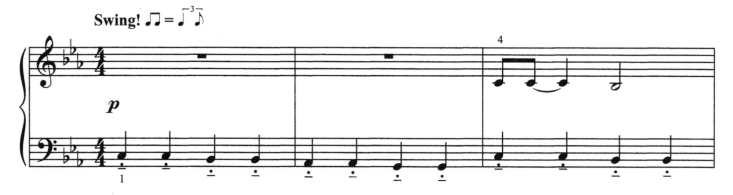

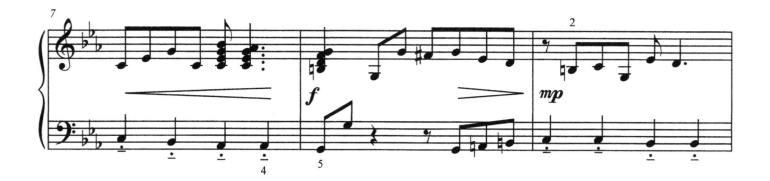

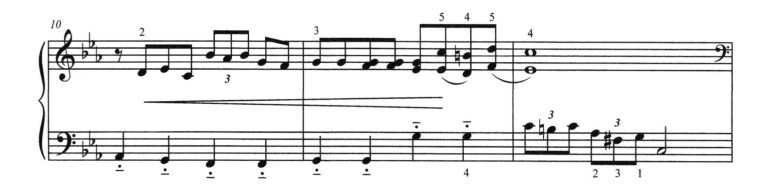

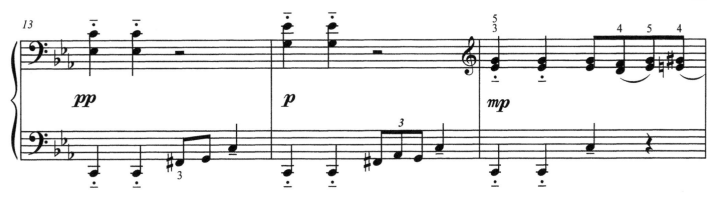

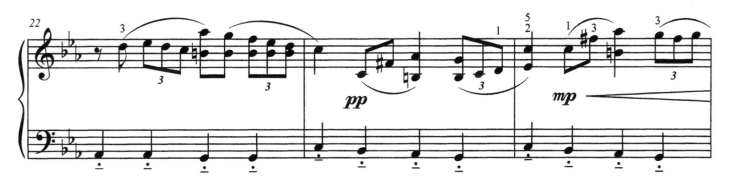

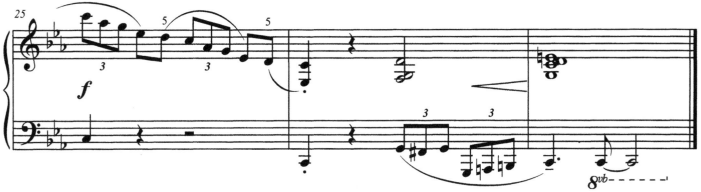

Stayin' Cool 2 / 2

Sun Flower Slow Drag

Scott Joplin
arr. Debra Wanless

Moderately

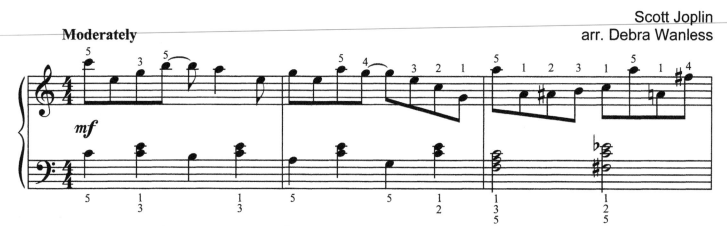

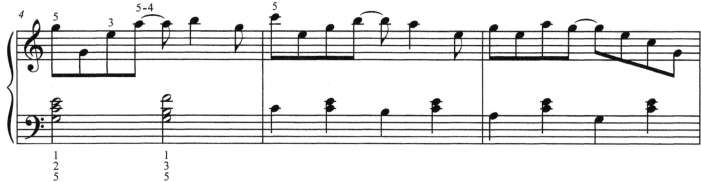

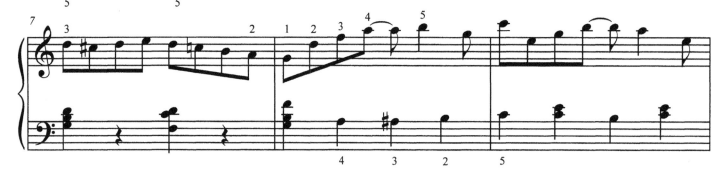

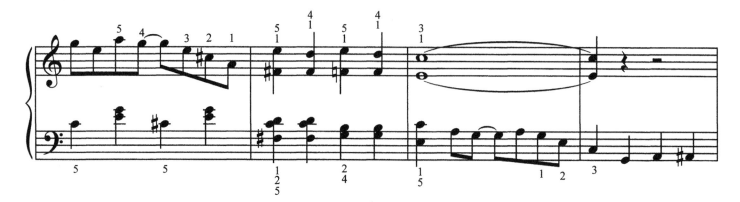

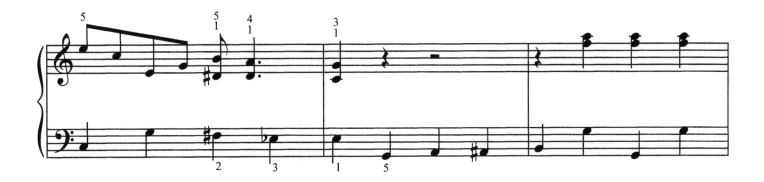

Sun Flower Slow Drag   2 / 2

Swamp Rock

David Story

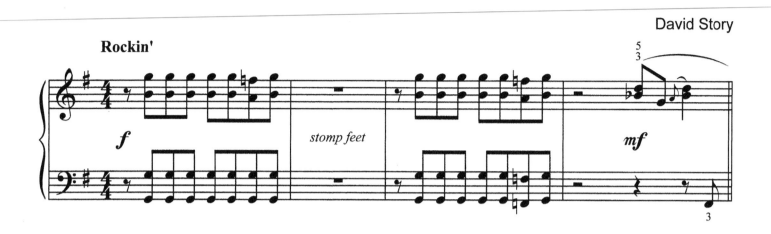

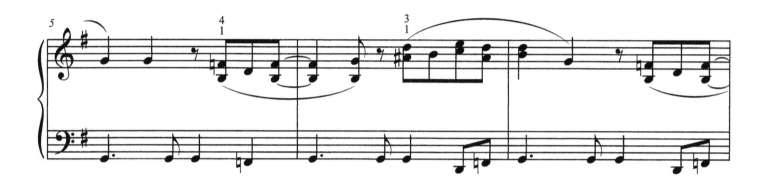

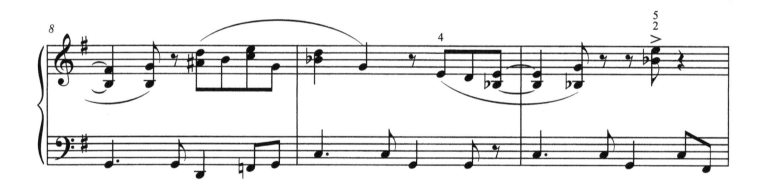

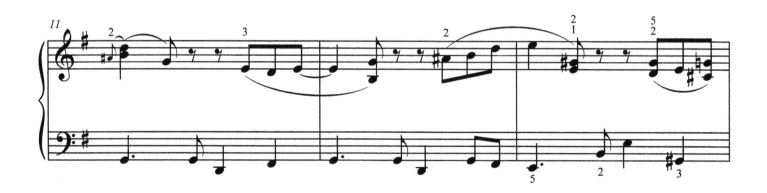

Swamp Rock   2 / 2

Tango For My Lovely Mom

Fishel Pustilnik

Steady Tango Beat

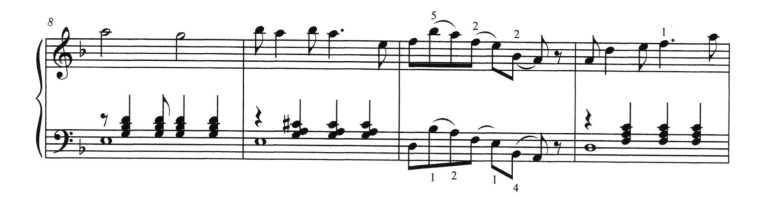

Tango For My Lovely Mom 2 / 2

The Moody B'ys

I'se the B'y That Builds the Boats

arr. Debra Wanless

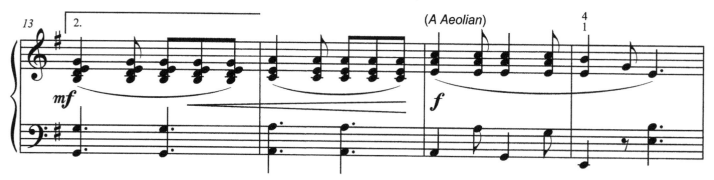

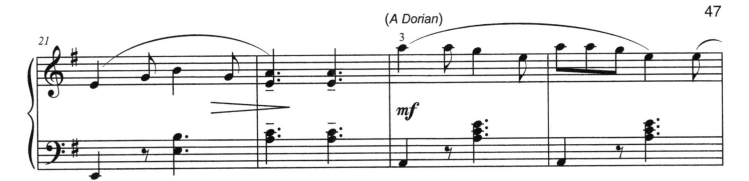

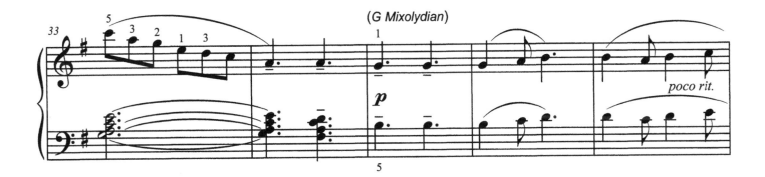

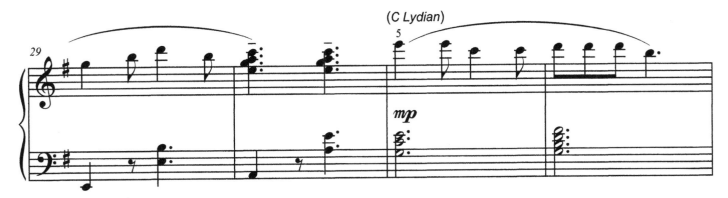

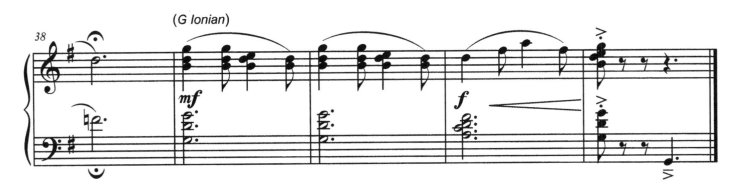

The Moody B'ys 2 / 2

Waltz of the Water Sprites

Sheila Tyrrell

Cheerfully